FREDRIK PAULÚN
KAROLIINA PAULÚN

LOW CARB HIGH QUALITY COOKBOOK

Recipes to Help You Lose Weight and Stay in Shape

Translated by Viktoria Lindback

SKYHORSE PUBLISHING

10 9 8 7 6 5 4 3 2 1

Library of Congress Cataloging-in-Publication Data is available on file.

ISBN: 978-1-62873-648-9

Printed in China

Contents

Paulún's LCHQ Food

LCHQ is a diet that has become incredibly popular in Sweden since it was launched with the book *Low Carb High Quality: Food for a Healthier, Thinner Life*. LCHQ can be described as the optimal diet for people who want to reduce their carbohydrate intake but not completely eliminate carbs from their diet. LCHQ stands for "Low Carbohydrate High Quality," and the diet consists of a carb intake of 20–30 percent energy (E%), depending on need. In comparison, the more extreme Low Carb High Fat (LCHF) diet advocates for a carbohydrate intake of 5–10 E%.

With LCHQ you'll find it's easier to exercise and keep your spirits up. LCHQ allows you to eat a lot of healthy ingredients, such as vegetables, nuts, and seeds, and reasonable amounts of root vegetables, whole grain products, legumes, fruits, and berries. The fat intake equals 40–50 E% and the focus is on scientifically proven healthy fats such as polyunsaturated fat, omega-3 fatty acids, and short-chain saturated fat. The protein intake is 20–30 E%, which fills you up, burns fat, and provides a terrific recovery when exercising.

LCHQ is first and foremost a lifestyle, not a diet. However, it is very easy to maintain your weight if you follow the LCHQ guidelines, since it consists of real ingredients that provide all of the necessary nutrients. Since there is a balance between nutrients and nothing is excluded, the body receives all the nutrients that it expends and there will be no surplus of anything. Nutritional content is the focus of LCHQ, since vitamins, minerals, and antioxidants are incredibly important for your health. LCHQ food is filled with these.

No Sugar Added

For me, LCHQ is a very good model to follow, especially since it eliminates refined sugar. If I eat sugar one day, I'll feel a distinct craving for more the next day, and if I don't break the habit immediately, it becomes increasingly more difficult to wean myself off it. I don't want to go so far as to say that I'm a sugar addict, which admittedly, many people are, but I do become accustomed to sugar. The reason is that sugar increases the release of ghrelin, a hormone that makes us hungry and crave sugar. The level of ghrelin slowly decreases when we don't eat sugar and after one to two weeks, it will reach a level that leaves us rather disinterested in sweetness. After that point, it's easier to resist sugar and keep to LCHQ. It's added sugar that's the

bad guy, not the sugar that you consume through fruit, berries, and honey, which all contain both slower carbohydrates and other nutrients.

The first few weeks on the LCHQ diet might leave you missing sugar if you're accustomed or addicted to it. Since it's a transitional phase, it's a small price to pay because sugar is one of the most dangerous things that humans consume. Plenty of research has found that the intake of sugar can increase the risk of cancer, cardiovascular disease, type-2 diabetes, inflammation, obesity, and caries.

Everyday LCHQ

I think it's very easy to follow LCHQ. The reasonable intake of carbohydrates keeps me from feeling drowsy after a meal and I never feel my blood sugar fluctuate. There are enough carbohydrates to satisfy me and generate enough energy for both physical and intellectual challenges.

In practice, it's also easy to eat out at a restaurant. I choose dishes that have a natural LCHQ composition, or I ask the chef to reduce the amount of carbohydrates and increase the amount of protein and fat. It comes naturally to me to choose carbohydrates with a low glycemic index, and meals with high levels of protein and fats of the highest quality. When I choose vegetables, it ought to be dishes with a rather high fat content, such as coleslaw, olive oil marinated

legumes, hummus, avocado salad, or something with olives. That way, I receive enough energy and super-quality fat.

In general, half of my plate usually consists of vegetables. A favorite of mine on the grocery list is frozen vegetables; they contain roughly an equal amount of nutrients as fresh veggies but are easier to cook, often cheaper, and are still delicious. When it comes to red meat, I eat it, but not to the same extent as other forms of meat such as fish, seafood, and poultry. If you eat red meat too frequently it can have a pro-inflammatory effect on the body; my general guideline is a maximum of three times a week. When there is the option, I always choose game instead of meat from livestock since it is leaner and healthier.

The Proper Ingredients

LCHQ relies on real ingredients and not products that pose as food. For example, powder sauce consists of extremely refined ingredients such as food enhancers, maltodextrin, and a plethora of other additives. Therefore, it's always better to make sauces from scratch based on more natural ingredients—crushed tomatoes or yogurt, for example. Or why not make your own mayonnaise?

I'm always shocked when I try to find good alternatives to home cooking. The last time I tried was when I was searching for frozen meatballs for my little son, in order to make him a quick lunch. The first thing that struck me was that they contained a higher fat content than those I could make on my own. The reason is, of course, that animal fat is a cheap surplus product. Additionally, every brand contained sugar and some type of flour,

often potato flour. These ingredients cause the carbohydrate content to skyrocket, the nutritional density decreases, and the number of empty calories increases. I finally decided to buy ground moose meat (an option in Sweden) to make my own and my son loved it.

Every LCHQ recipe relies on real ingredients, so prepare to purchase root vegetables, meat, chicken, vegetables, fish, seafood, spices, etc. The spices are particularly interesting since they not only add flavor to the food but also have a bunch of other healthy characteristics. Many spices are also extremely rich in antioxidants and can improve your digestion, serve antibacterial purposes, and inhibit inflammation. Some are even as effective as medicine, one example being cinnamon, which can help balance your blood sugar.

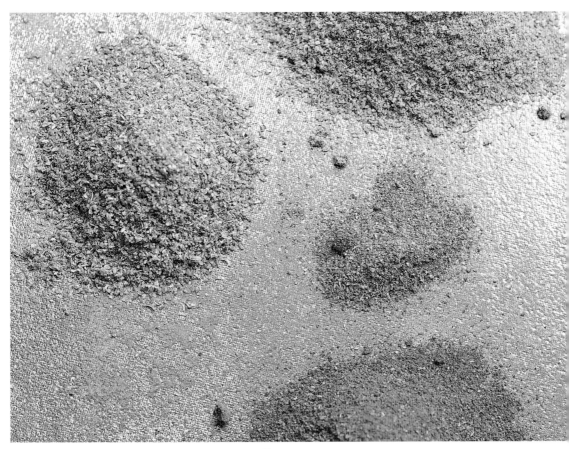

LCHQ and the Interests of Animals

For me, ethical treatment of animals is a major concern. Few issues are as important to me as the assurance that the animals we eat suffer as little as possible and are healthy for as long as they live. From that perspective, game meat is a great alternative, although it is not readily available to everyone. When I must buy beef from the grocery store, I try to buy organic. As a consumer, this assures me that the animals spent some time outside and I know that there are more stringent rules for how large their enclosures and cages have to be. It also means that the animals have not been subjected to arbitrary doses of antibiotics, which is, of course, important in order to inhibit the resistance to antibiotics that is threatening the longterm health of mankind.

Organic eggs are an obvious choice for me, since the chickens lead better lives and the eggs are healthier for you. On average, they contain higher levels of vitamins and minerals, and I also think they taste better.

I also choose organic dairy products as often as possible. Studies have shown that these contain more omega-3 fats compared to their conventionally produced equivalents.

Not Just Food

The Q in LCHQ is not only an abbreviation for nutrition of highest quality but also for quality of life. This implies a focus on enjoyment and well-being. The LCHQ lifestyle is not something you should have to endure; it's something you should experience and enjoy! That means coffee, tea, red wine, and other pleasures are allowed, as long as they are consumed in reasonable amounts. Both red wine and caffeinated drinks generate the reward substance dopamine, which gives a feeling of pleasure and desire. A simplified description is that dopamine can be considered "the meaning of life." If we do not receive dopamine, we end up feeling low and depressed, and can even lose the will to live. Good food also generates dopamine, which is the reason LCHQ focuses on flavors and enjoyable food experiences.

Since few things benefit the quality of life as much as exercise, working out is an important aspect of living the LCHQ lifestyle. Thanks to the diet's inclusion of the proper number of carbohydrates to make your muscles function, it is perfectly fine to combine LCHQ with exercise. Working out not only generates dopamine but also serotonin and endorphins, which contribute to happiness, quality of life, and well-being. I will discuss the benefits of exercise later in the book.

For the Whole Family

As you can see, LCHQ is not a weight loss diet or an extreme diet that deprives you of nutrients. This ensures that the whole family can eat LCHQ food regardless of goals. It's simply a question of eating high-quality food prepared from the best ingredients. Since you are always eating enough to feel full, there is no calorie restriction, which also contributes to quality of life.

The diet is based on ingredients that provide a better sense of fullness per calorie and not energy dense, sugared products or intermediaries. Twenty to thirty percent carbohydrates might not be enough for all children, especially not rambunctious ones, but then it's easy to increase the amount.

You can choose to either increase the amount of carbs in the recipes, through whole grain oats, for example, or by simply giving them extra fruit after dinner. This way, the number of carbs is absolutely enough for their growth, brain development, and physical activity. The base recipes are, however, adjusted to fit everyone's needs.

Another important aspect for those of you with children is that kindergartens and schools rarely provide food of LCHQ quality. This isn't a huge worry as long as you feed them LCHQ at home as much as possible. After all, it is not a weight loss diet or religion; it's simply an effort to obtain as much nutrition as possible.

Better Exercise with Proper Food

When you follow the LCHQ diet, it's also wise to dedicate yourself to regular physical activity in order to increase your quality of life. You will become more attractive, faster, stronger, more agile, and also happier! Plenty of studies show that people who eat well and exercise regularly deem their quality of life to be better than others', so the Q is relevant even here. Exercising also provides a large number of health benefits.

Studies have found that the more muscle tissue a person has, the higher their life expectancy usually is. Exercise combined with LCHQ generates more muscle and more developed body tissue that absorbs blood sugar and burns fat. Besides the obvious aesthetic appeal of lots of muscle and little fat, it also contributes to a reduced risk for type-2 diabetes and cardiovascular disease. Muscles help push the blood through the blood vessels, which directly helps reduce the pressure on the heart. The easier you make the heart's job, the better you will feel and you will also live longer. One evident but often disregarded effect of a developed muscular structure is that your body can better handle physical challenges. For example, if you're unlucky enough to get into a car accident, the risk of serious injuries is much lower if you have a good muscle mass. Even the risk of cancer, dementia, sleep disorders, and depression can be reduced if you exercise according to the LCHQ guidelines.

Is LCHQ the Equivalent of the Caveman Diet?

I have previously written a book about the Caveman diet and I have a positive view of the part such food can play in our modern diet. However, the answer to the question above is no, but there are some similarities. The distribution of nutrients in LCHQ is very similar to the Caveman diet. They also share the belief that the ingredients should be of high quality, and that the diet should contain a lot of omega-3 fat and relatively low amounts of long-chained saturated fat. Surely humans ate a lot of meat back in the day, but game generally contains lower amounts of fat (since the animals are constantly on the move) and the saturated fat's share of the total fat content is lower. Both diets also advocate for the elimination of refined sugar and destroyed fats (which can occur through exposure to heat or industrial processing).

In contrast to the Caveman diet, LCHQ does not strictly prohibit dairy products or gluten. It's not dangerous in any way to consume these substances, unless you are allergic or intolerant. It's actually quite the opposite; milk products are very nutritious. For example, cheese, cottage cheese, and Greek yogurt are high-quality sources of protein, as well as excellent sources of vitamin B12 for vegetarians. Whole grain wheat products, barley, and rye contain gluten, which does not pose a problem as long as you are not overly sensitive. Whole grain products are generally very healthy since they contain high levels of vitamins and minerals, as well as many antioxidants and fibers that strengthen the intestinal flora.

LCHQ and the Diabetic

In Sweden, there are approximately 70,000 type-1 diabetics, while the U.S. has a number closer to 1.29 million. This form of diabetes is an autoimmune disease where the body lacks the ability to produce insulin, for which the diabetic can compensate by scheduling insulin injections. Type-1 diabetes can occur at any point, but it is likely to develop early on in life, which is why it is often referred to as "Juvenile Diabetes." It is therefore incredibly important to keep a good diet. Doing so will enable the diabetic to balance their blood sugar levels and reduce the risk for related diseases.

The same is true for type-2 diabetes, even if it is a type of diabetes that occurs later in life. The disease is characterized by a reduced sensitivity to insulin and diminished functionality of the existing insulin. You can both prevent and treat type-2 diabetes. Regardless of which type you suffer from, LCHQ is a great diet. The combination of low levels of carbohydrates and low glycemic index automatically reduces the amount of blood sugar you have to deal with. At the same time, the intake is not low enough to risk further reducing your insulin sensitivity, which is a risk if you completely eliminate carbohydrates.

We also know that antioxidants are a diabetic's best friend, since they protect against some of the harm caused by elevated blood sugar levels. Fat and protein help diabetics since it provides a slower digestion and therefore more even blood sugar levels and a better sense of fullness. The fact that LCHQ only includes real ingredients also contributes to better health, even for those without diabetes. For recently diagnosed type-2 diabetics, I would argue that LCHQ in combination with regular physical activity can actually make the disease retract. In that regard, food can serve as medicine.

LCHQ

BREAKFAST

Cottage Cheese with Raspberries, Roasted Pumpkin Seeds,
and Almond Flakes

Cottage Cheese with Apple, Cinnamon, and Hazelnuts

Cottage Cheese with Almonds and Fruit

Nut and Seed Granola

Golden Oat Granola

Strawberry and Basil Smoothie

Blueberry and Almond Smoothie

Chocolate and Banana Smoothie

Scrambled Eggs with Spinach and Salmon

Cottage Cheese with Raspberries, Roasted Pumpkin Seeds, and Almond Flakes

1 serving

2 tbsp pumpkin seeds
2 tbsp almond flakes
1 tsp honey
⅔ cup (150 ml) raspberries
½ cup (125 g) cottage cheese

▶ Roast the pumpkin seeds and almond flakes in a hot, nonstick frying pan for about 30 seconds. Drizzle honey over the raspberries, add the cottage cheese, and top off with the roasted pumpkin seeds and sliced almonds.

Cottage cheese is a dairy aisle favorite. The protein content is very high, and the fat content is both reasonable and of good quality. Research has shown that dairy fat is better for your health and weight than previously thought. Pumpkin seeds are some of the most protein rich seeds and they contain a high amount of antioxidants. Additionally, the raspberries contain veritable blasts of antioxidants with a low glycemic index.

15

Cottage Cheese with Apple, Cinnamon, and Hazelnuts

1 serving

1 apple
½ tsp ground cinnamon
½ cup (125 g) cottage cheese
3½ tbsp (50 ml) chopped, roasted hazelnuts

▶ Split the apple, remove the core, and dice the apple flesh. Sprinkle cinnamon on top and heat the apple in the microwave until it softens, about ½–1 minute. Top off with the cottage cheese and chopped hazelnuts.

Hazelnuts are very healthy. They contain high levels of magnesium and their flavor goes wonderfully with apple and cinnamon. Cinnamon has been found to help balance the blood sugar and reduce blood fats, and also contains an incredible amount of antioxidants! Cinnamon's ORAC (oxygen radical absorption capacity) value is 250,000, which could be compared to such things as blueberries, which have a value of approximately 10,000.

Cottage Cheese with Almonds and Fruit

1 serving

20 sweet almonds
1 tbsp coconut flakes
1 tbsp cacao nibs or cocoa powder
7 oz (200 g) cottage cheese
½ banana
3½ tbsp (50 ml) blueberries

▶ Coarsely chop the almonds and mix them with the coconut, cacao nibs, and cottage cheese. Slice the banana and place on top along with the blueberries.

Cottage cheese is a highly protein-rich product and a decent source of fat with a high level of SCT and MCT (short and medium-chained saturated fats, respectively). As opposed to LCT (long-chained saturated fats), SCT and MCT make it easier to maintain your weight while also reducing the risk for cardiovascular disease and type-2 diabetes. Cacao nibs are a delightful ingredient that provide fat, antioxidants, protein, and a crunchy texture. They also taste delicious!

Nut and Seed Granola

10 servings

2⅛ cups (500 ml) walnuts
¾ cup (200 ml) hazelnuts
2 cups (500 ml) buckwheat flakes
¾ cup (200 ml) goji berries
10 tbsp pumpkin seeds
5 tbsp crushed flaxseed
3 tbsp cacao nibs

For serving
cottage cheese yogurt (1 cup [200 ml] plain yogurt
+ ¼ cup [50 ml] cottage cheese)
fresh raspberries and other berries

▶ Chop the nuts and mix with the rest of the ingredients. One serving is about ½ cup (100 ml). The cottage cheese yogurt is a great addition. Feel free to sprinkle some raspberries or other berries on top.

LCHQ granola offers a great sense of satiety. The goji berries provide this meal with an exceptionally high number of antioxidants.

Golden Oat Granola

5 servings

1 cup (100 g) pecans
2 tbsp canola oil
2 tbsp honey
¾ cup (200 ml) oatmeal
3½ tbsp (50 ml) sunflower seeds
3½ tbsp (50 ml) peeled sesame seeds
3½ tbsp (50 ml) pumpkin seeds
a pinch of ground cinnamon
a pinch of ground cardamom
3½ tbsp (50 ml) raisins

For serving
plain yogurt

▶ Preheat the oven to 350°F (175°C). Coarsely chop the pecans. Heat the oil and honey in a saucepan. Remove the pan from the stove, and then add the oatmeal, chopped nuts, fruit, and spices. Mix well. Spread out the mixture on a baking sheet lined with parchment paper. Roast in the middle of the oven for about 15 minutes or until the granola turns golden. Stir occasionally while roasting, since it burns easily.

Let the granola cool, add the raisins, and store in an airtight container. The granola will keep for a couple of weeks.

Serve with plain yogurt.

Here we have gathered some of the best ingredients the grocery store has to offer. Oatmeal is very rich in good fats, protein, and antioxidants. It's also gluten free and has a low glycemic index. Adding fruit and nuts to an oatmeal-based granola lowers the glycemic index significantly and contributes to your health with large amounts of antioxidants, minerals, vitamins, and healthy fats.

Strawberry and Basil Smoothie

1 serving

½ cup (100 g) cottage cheese
¾ cup (200 ml) milk
½ cup (100 ml) strawberries
½ avocado
5 basil leaves

▶ Combine all of the ingredients in a blender until it becomes a smooth drink.

This is a well-balanced smoothie with high-quality fat from avocado, protein from cottage cheese and milk, along with slow carbohydrates from the strawberries. Basil provides a fresh taste and also contributes a large amount of antioxidants.

Blueberry and Almond Smoothie

1 serving

⅔ cup (150 g) cottage cheese
⅔ cup (150 ml) oat milk
½ cup (100 ml) frozen blueberries
3½ tbsp (50 ml) sweet almonds

▶ Combine all of the ingredients in a blender until it becomes a smooth drink.

Here we get super healthy blueberries along with the best source of fat there is: almonds!

Chocolate and Banana Smoothie

1 serving

1 banana
4.4 oz (125 g) Silken tofu
⅓ cup (75 ml) coconut milk
⅔–¾ cup (150–200 ml) water
1 tbsp cocoa powder
3½ tbsp (50 ml) walnuts

▶ Slice the banana and let it sit in the freezer for a couple of hours. Combine with the rest of the ingredients in a blender until it becomes a smooth drink.

This is an easy vegan smoothie that doesn't contain dairy products. Instead, it gets protein from tofu and fat from coconut and walnuts. The super healthy cocoa powder provides flavor, minerals, and enormous amounts of antioxidants. Walnuts have a very good fat profile that not only boosts the brain and fat burning processes, but also seems to positively affect sperm quality in males. Walnuts also provide some protein and antioxidants.

Scrambled Eggs with Spinach and Salmon

1 serving

½ red onion
1 tbsp canola oil
a handful of spinach
2 eggs
salt
freshly ground black pepper

For serving
1 slice of smoked salmon
1 glass of tomato juice
1 apple, sliced

▶ Peel and chop the onion. Heat the oil in a frying pan, add the onion and spinach and fry at medium heat until the liquid evaporates. Crack the eggs and stir with a wooden spoon until the eggs have solidified. Add salt and pepper to taste.

Serve with smoked salmon, tomato juice, and apple slices.

This is a very versatile favorite that works well as breakfast, a snack, or as lunch. When buying eggs, make sure they are organic. The FDA has examined all types of eggs and the organic ones generally contain more of almost every nutrient. Tomato juice is a great source of the antioxidant lycopene, which protects against such things as prostate and breast cancer, and improves the body's natural ability to protect against the sun.

LCHQ

SOUP

Salmon Soup with Shrimp and Tomato

Fish Soup with Red Curry

Chicken Soup with Coconut and Mushroom

Chicken Soup with Curry

Chicken Soup with Chickpeas and Yogurt

Mexican Meat Soup

Salmon Soup with Shrimp and Tomato

4 servings

2 onions
3 tbsp olive oil
2 cans of crushed tomatoes (approx. 28 oz [800 g] total)
3½ cups (800 ml) water
4 tbsp concentrated fish stock
½ cup (100 ml) frozen chopped dill
1.3 lbs (600 g) skinless salmon fillet, cubed
7 oz (200 g) peeled shrimp
freshly ground black pepper

▶ Peel and chop the onion. Heat the oil in a pan, add the onion, and fry for a short while. Add the crushed tomatoes, water, stock, and dill and bring to a boil for about 10 minutes. Add the salmon and let simmer for another 2 minutes. Add the shrimp and add pepper to taste.

A perfect dinner for the whole family, even if not everyone follows LCHQ. Let those who want more carbs eat a couple of slices of dark whole grain bread in addition to the soup. Salmon is a first-class source of omega-3 fats, which are known for protecting against cardiovascular disease and various types of inflammation. Soup also tends to be a good way of consuming nutrients. Eating soup makes you full off of fewer calories compared to solid food, since it's both hot and provides a lot of liquid.

Fish Soup with Red Curry

4 servings

(400 g) Pollock fillet
1 onion
2 garlic cloves, pressed
14 oz (400 g) carrots
10½ oz (300 g) parsley root
2 tbsp canola oil
2 tbsp red curry paste
3 cups (700 ml) water
2 tbsp concentrated fish stock
1 can of coconut milk (14 oz [400 g])

For serving
fresh cilantro

▶ Cut the fish into cubes. Peel and chop the onion. Peel and dice the carrots and parsley root.

Heat the oil in a large saucepan, then add the onion and garlic and fry for a couple of minutes. Add the carrots, parsley root, and curry paste and fry for a few minutes more. Pour in the water and fish stock, bring to a boil, and let boil for about 10 minutes. Add the coconut milk, bring to a boil, and then add the fish. Let simmer for 2–3 minutes. Add fresh, chopped cilantro to taste.

Pollock is a very lean, white fish that still contains enough omega-3 fats to have a good health benefit. In addition, fish protein positively affects insulin sensitivity and lowers blood pressure. The coconut milk in this dish is not only delicious but also contains fatty acids, which are easy for the body to burn off, making it easier to maintain your weight.

Chicken Soup with Coconut and Mushroom

4 servings

1 lb (500 g) chicken thigh fillets
1 stalk of lemongrass
4 carrots
14 oz (400 g) mushrooms
3 tbsp canola oil
1 can of coconut milk (14 oz [400 g])
3 cups (700 ml) water
2 tbsp green curry paste
2 tbsp Thai fish sauce
14 oz (400 g) frozen broccoli florets

▶ Slice the chicken fillets, pound the hard part of the lemongrass stalk, and finely shred it. Peel the carrots and slice into small coins. Slice the mushrooms.

Heat the oil in a saucepan. Add the chicken and lemongrass and fry for a couple of minutes. Add the carrots and mushroom and continue to fry for a while longer. Add the coconut milk, water, curry paste, and fish sauce and bring to a boil. Add the broccoli florets and let everything simmer for an additional 2–3 minutes until the chicken is cooked through.

Chicken is a great source of protein and a good alternative to red meat, which appears to increase the risk for cardiovascular disease and several forms of cancer if consumed in large amounts.

Chicken Soup with Curry

4 servings

1 lb (500 g) ground chicken
1 onion
1 red chili
3 tbsp canola oil
2 tsp mango curry or yellow curry
5 cups (1.2 liters) water
2 chicken bouillon cubes
2¾ cups (150 g) mushrooms
1 squash

▶ Roll the chicken into small balls. Peel and chop the onion. Split, remove the core, and finely shred the chili.

Heat the oil in a pan, add the onions, chili, curry, and let fry for a couple of minutes. Add the water and bouillon and bring to a boil. Add the chicken balls and boil for approximately 5 minutes. Split the mushrooms and dice the squash and add to the soup. Let boil for an additional 5 minutes.

Ground chicken is an underrated ingredient. It's rich in protein and is delicious, cheap, and easy to cook. Chicken combined with a large amount of mushrooms and squash makes this a very filling dish with few calories.

Chicken Soup with Chickpeas and Yogurt

4 servings

1 onion
10½ oz (300 g) parsnip
2 celery stalks
1 red pepper
1 lb (500 g) chicken thigh fillets
4 tbsp canola oil
2 garlic cloves, pressed
1 tsp ground cumin
1 tsp paprika
1 tsp cayenne pepper
3 cups (700 ml) water
1 can of crushed tomatoes (14 oz [400 g])
2 tbsp concentrated chicken stock
2 tbsp tomato purée
1⅓ cup (300 ml) boiled chickpeas

For serving
4 tbsp Greek yogurt

▶ Peel and chop the onion. Peel and dice the parsnips and slice the celery stalks. Dice the pepper. Dice the chicken fillets.

Heat the oil in a saucepan and add the onion and garlic. Fry for a short while. Add the chicken and sear it. Add the vegetables and spices, and then continue to fry for a while. Add the water, diced tomatoes, stock, and tomato puree. Bring to a boil and let cook for about 10 minutes. Rinse the chickpeas and add to the soup. Feel free to serve with a little bit of Greek yogurt on the plate.

The thigh fillet is the tastiest part of the chicken. The flavorful meat goes well with heavy spices, as in this recipe. When crushed tomatoes are heated, the antioxidants penetrate the core and the skin, so the sauce becomes extra nutritious.

Mexican Meat Soup

4 servings

2 red onions
4 tbsp canola oil
1 lb (500 g) ground beef, 90% lean
½ tsp ground cumin
½ tsp ground cilantro
½ tsp cayenne pepper
½ tsp paprika
3½ cups (800 ml) water
1 can of crushed tomatoes (14 oz [400 g])
2 meat bouillon cubes
¾ cup (200 ml) frozen corn
¾ cup (200 ml) frozen kidney beans

▶ Peel and finely chop the onion. Heat the oil in a saucepan, add the ground beef, chopped onion, and spices and sear the mixture. Add the water, crushed tomato, and bouillon cubes. Bring to a boil and let cook for approximately 10 minutes. Add the corn and beans and let them heat up in the soup.

Spices, spices, and more spices—not only do they eliminate the need for additives and contribute with a myriad of antioxidants, they're usually also antibacterial and inhibit inflammations. Soup is a rather remarkable meal in many ways. Those who require more carbs can easily eat the soup with high-quality bread.

LCHQ

SALAD

Chicken Caesar Salad with Tomatoes

Tuna Salad with Ajvar Relish

Chicken Salad with Beets and Feta Cream

Mackerel Salad with Whole Grain Oats and Egg

Chicken Salad with Whole Grain Oats and Avocado

Thai Salad with Shrimp and Quinoa

Salmon Salad Niçoise

Tex-Mex Chicken Salad

Chicken Caesar Salad with Tomatoes

4 servings

1¾ lb (800 g) chicken fillets
2 tbsp olive oil
salt
freshly ground black pepper

Caesar Dressing
4 pickled anchovy fillets
1 garlic clove, pressed
1 tbsp freshly squeezed lemon juice
1 egg yolk
a pinch of black pepper
½ cup (125 ml) olive oil
3½ tbsp (50 ml) grated Parmesan

For serving
10½ oz (300 g) romaine lettuce
14 oz (400 g) grape tomatoes

▶ Preheat the oven to 400°F (200°C). Place the chicken fillets in a baking dish. Drizzle with olive oil and season with salt and pepper. Bake in the oven for approximately 30 minutes or until the fillets are cooked through. Let the meat cool and then slice it thinly.

Finely chop the anchovies and blend them with the garlic, lemon juice, egg yolk, and black pepper in a food processor or blender. Add the oil in a thin stream so the dressing doesn't "break." Stir in the Parmesan cheese.

Chop the lettuce, add the dressing, and mix well in a large salad bowl. Serve with the tomatoes and sliced chicken.

Romaine lettuce is one of the darker and deeper green varieties of lettuce. The color actually proves that romaine lettuce is very rich in folic acid and antioxidants. And speaking of dressing, did you know that there is more protein in an egg yolk than in an egg white?

Tuna Salad with Ajvar Relish

2 servings

1 can of tuna in oil (5 oz [150 g])
4 tbsp Greek yogurt
2 tbsp ajvar relish (spicy)
2 avocados
1 orange bell pepper
2 boiled eggs
¾ cup (200 ml) frozen green peas
10½ oz (300 g) romaine lettuce
salt
freshly ground black pepper

▶ Drain the can of tuna and mix with the yogurt and ajvar relish. Season with salt and pepper to taste.

Slice the avocados and bell pepper. Peel and cut the egg into wedges. Bring a pot of water to a bowl and pour it over the green peas. Let the peas sit for a minute and then drain out the water.

Place the romaine lettuce and the other vegetables on plates and top off with the tuna mix and egg wedges.

Even canned tuna is healthy! The fish not only has low cholesterol, but is rich in Omega-3 fatty acids. Tuna salad combines well with many other beneficial ingredients. Frozen peas are a cheap and delicious source of protein.

Chicken Salad with Beets and Feta Cream

4 servings

1⅓ lbs (600 g) chicken fillets
4 tbsp olive oil
1 organic lemon, zest
lemon pepper seasoning
10½ oz (300 g) red beets
10½ oz (300 g) yellow beets
10½ oz (300 g) romaine lettuce
2½ oz (70 g) arugula
1 tbsp red wine vinegar
salt
freshly ground black pepper

Feta Cream
5⅓ oz (150 g) feta cheese
3½ tbsp (100 ml) plain Greek yogurt
freshly ground black pepper

▶ Preheat the oven to 400°F (200°C). Place the chicken fillets in a baking dish. Mix 2 tbsp of the oil with the lemon zest and pour over the chicken. Add salt and pepper, and rub the fillets so the oil and spices get all over the chicken. Bake the fillets in the oven for about 30 minutes or until they are cooked through.

Bring the beets to a boil in two separate saucepans for 45–50 minutes or until they are fully cooked. Let them cool, and then peel and dice them.

Distribute the lettuce on plates. Add the diced beets, 2 tbsp of oil, vinegar, salt, and pepper. Slice the chicken fillets and place on top of the salad. Mash the feta cheese with a fork, mix in the yogurt, and add black pepper to taste. Serve the salad with the feta cream.

Tip! This salad also works well with a dressing based on yogurt, lemon zest, pressed garlic, salt, and pepper. The feta cheese can then be sprinkled on top of the salad.

Root vegetables are rich in antioxidants and contain substances that inhibit cancer development. They're also pretty much calorie free so they can be consumed limitlessly. Acid lowers the pH-level, which in turn generates a lower glycemic index, so both red wine vinegar and lemon serve their function in this recipe.

Mackerel Salad with Whole Grain Oats and Egg

4 servings

¾ cup (200 ml) uncooked whole grain oats
2 avocados
10½ oz (300 g) cherry tomatoes
1 bunch of radishes
1 red onion
¾ cup (200 ml) frozen green peas
3½ oz (100 g) mixed lettuce and herbs
(e.g., baby spinach, arugula, dill, parsley, chives, basil)
2 tbsp olive oil
2 tbsp balsamic vinegar
4 boiled eggs
14 oz (400 g) smoked mackerel fillets (preferably
seasoned with pepper)
salt
freshly ground black pepper

▶ Rinse and boil the whole grain oats according to the directions on the packaging. Pit and dice the avocados, wedge the tomatoes, and slice the radishes and onion.

Bring the water to a boil and add the frozen peas. Pour out the water immediately.

Mix the vegetables, whole grain oats, and fish with the salad and fresh herbs. Add oil and vinegar, stir, and add salt and pepper to taste. Split the eggs in halves and place them on top of the salad, along with the mackerel.

Whole grain oats are the perfect source of carb in a salad because of their low glycemic index and highly nutritional characteristics. The water soluble fibers form a gel in the stomach and intestines, which provides a better sense of satiety and a slower absorbency of blood sugar. Mackerel is one of the most cost-effective types of fish, and in this form it's really easy to use. The omega-3 content in smoked mackerel is equivalent to that of fresh mackerel.

Chicken Salad with Whole Grain Oats and Avocado

4 servings

1 lb (500 g) chicken fillet
4 tbsp olive oil
¾ cup (200 ml) uncooked whole grain oats
4 avocados
10½ oz (300 g) cherry tomatoes
1 red onion
3½ oz (100 g) mixed lettuce, e.g., frisee lettuce, arugula, and mache lettuce
1 tbsp balsamic vinegar
salt
freshly ground black pepper

▶ Preheat the oven to 400°F (200°C). Place the chicken fillets in a baking dish, rub them with 2 tbsp of olive oil and salt and pepper. Bake in the oven for approximately 30 minutes or until they are cooked through.

Rinse the whole grain oats and boil according to the directions on the packaging. Pit and dice the avocados and cut the tomatoes into wedges.

Peel the onions and cut into thin slices. Mix the whole grain oats, avocado, and tomato wedges with the lettuce. Add 2 tbsp of the oil and the vinegar and stir. Season with salt and pepper to taste.

Slice the chicken fillets and serve with the salad.

The lean chicken fillets provide a perfect nutritional intake when paired with the more fatty avocado and olive oil. This is a large serving of lettuce, which provides both wonderful color to the meal and is a food with few calories, but it's also a healthy dose of folic acid and antioxidants. Whole grain oats are also a perfect rice substitute.

Thai Salad with Shrimp and Quinoa

4 servings

½ cup (100 ml) uncooked black quinoa
4 avocados
1 cucumber
3 oz (80 g) chives
½ lb (250 g) poached shrimp, peeled and rinsed
2½ oz (70 g) mache lettuce
4 hardboiled eggs

Dressing
1 red chili
4 tbsp olive oil
1 tbsp freshly squeezed lime juice
2 tbsp chopped fresh cilantro
1 tsp Thai fish sauce

▶ Boil the quinoa according to the directions on the packaging.

Split the chili in half lengthwise, remove the seeds, and thinly slice it. Mix with the rest of the ingredients for the dressing.

Pit and dice the avocados. Peel the cucumber, split it vertically, scrape out the core with a spoon and dice the remains. Finely chop the chives. Mix the shrimp, quinoa, vegetables, and lettuce. Pour the dressing on top and stir. Halve the eggs and place atop the salad.

In terms of antioxidants, black quinoa is the richest type of this fantastic, low-glycemic product. Shrimp is almost always good to keep in the refrigerator, since it's delicious and is a high-quality source of protein stuffed with nutrients. The iodine content is high and the pink color stems from the antioxidant astaxanthin.

58

Salmon Salad Niçoise

4 servings

1¾ lbs (800 g) salmon fillet
3½ oz (100 g) green beans
4 hardboiled eggs
9 oz (250 g) cherry tomatoes
1 red onion
5⅓ oz (150 g) mixed lettuce, e.g., arugula and mache
(200 g) canned artichoke hearts
16 anchovy fillets
20 black olives
3 tbsp olive oil
1 tbsp red wine vinegar
salt
freshly ground black pepper

▶ Set the oven to 400°F (200°C). Place the salmon skin-side up in a baking dish and bake for 20 minutes. Remove the skin and salt the salmon.

Boil the green beans in salted water for 2 minutes. Cut the eggs into wedges, half the tomatoes, and peel and thinly slice the red onion. Place the lettuce on four plates and distribute all ingredients on top. Top with oil and vinegar. Add salt and pepper to taste.

A salad Niçoise usually contains tuna, but isn't salmon a tastier fish? I think most people would agree, and besides, the omega-3 content is much higher. This low-carb LCHQ recipe is great for late-night dinners just before bed, because you don't need a lot of carbohydrates when you're sleeping.

Tex-Mex Chicken Salad

4 servings

1 lb (500 g) chicken fillets
3 tbsp olive oil
4 avocados
9 oz (250 g) tomatoes
1 red onion
¾ cup (200 ml) boiled kidney beans
¾ cup (200 ml) boiled black beans
¾ cup (200 ml) corn
a small head of iceberg lettuce
½ tbsp red wine vinegar
salt
freshly ground black pepper

Tomato Salsa
1 can of crushed tomatoes (14 oz [400 g])
2–3 tbsp chopped fresh cilantro
1 tbsp olive oil
1 garlic clove, pressed
salt
freshly ground black pepper

For serving
¾ cup (200 ml) sour cream

▶ Preheat the oven to 400°F (200°C). Place the chicken fillets in a baking dish and rub them with one tablespoon of oil and salt and pepper. Bake in the oven for 20–25 minutes until they are cooked all the way through. Thinly slice the meat.

Scrape out the flesh of the avocados and tomatoes and then dice them. Peel and finely chop the onion. Mix all of the salad ingredients together with the chicken. Pour in 2 tablespoons of oil and the vinegar. Add salt and pepper to taste. You can choose to either chop the lettuce and mix with the rest of the ingredients or use the lettuce leaves as a wrap.

Mix all of the ingredients for the tomato salsa and add salt and pepper to taste.

Serve the chicken salad with the tomato salsa and sour cream on the side.

Chicken is a very tasty and cost-effective source of protein, but since it's quite lean it requires a lot of fat in order for the flavors to seep through. Some of the best sources of fat are avocado and olive oil. This recipe also includes two of the most antioxidant rich legumes—black beans and kidney beans. LCHQ recommends between 20–30 E% of carbohydrates depending on need, and the more physically active you are, the more you will need. This recipe contains about 20 percent carbohydrates.

LCHQ

FISH AND SEAFOOD

Oven-baked Salmon with Vegetables and Lemon-Thyme Sauce

Oven-baked Salmon with Asparagus, Tomatoes, and Olives

Cod on a Bed of Greens

Cod with Garlic-fried Mushrooms and Quinoa

Poached Salmon with Quinoa and Cilantro Yogurt

Salmon Sashimi with Bok Choy and Pine Nuts

Almond-breaded Halibut with Hot Lentil Salad

Salmon with Ratatouille and Saffron Yogurt

Oven-baked Salmon with Vegetables and Lemon-Thyme Sauce

4 servings

1⅓ lbs (600 g) salmon fillet
14 oz (400 g) broccoli
1 small head of lettuce (18 oz [500 g])
4 carrots
2 red bell peppers

Lemon-Thyme Sauce
½ cup (125 g) crème fraiche
1½ tbsp mayonnaise
2 tsp fresh thyme leaves
1 tsp organic lemon zest
salt
freshly ground white pepper

▶ Preheat the oven to 400°F (200°C). Place the salmon in a baking dish skin-side up and bake for about 20 minutes. Peel off the skin.

Split the broccoli and cauliflower into small florets. Peel the carrots and cut them into sticks. Halve, scrape out, and slice the bell pepper. Bring water to a boil in a saucepan, add the carrots, and let them boil for 2 minutes. Add the broccoli and cauliflower and let boil for an additional minute. Add the pepper and let boil for another minute, then pour out the water.

Mix the ingredients for the sauce and add salt and pepper to taste. Salt the salmon to taste.

This is how you use vegetables as a real ingredient and not just as garnish. This recipe contains mixed brassicas, which have documented cancer-retarding properties, with peppers and carrots, which are real carotenoid bombs. Carotenoids are a particular type of antioxidant that is known to prevent the cholesterol in blood from going rancid and thus reduces the risk for cardiovascular disease.

Oven-baked Salmon with Asparagus, Tomatoes, and Olives

4 servings

1⅓ lbs (600 g) skinless salmon fillet
2 bunches of green asparagus (approx. 14 oz [400 g])
4 tbsp olive oil
14 oz (400 g) plum tomatoes
30 black olives, preferably kalamata
1 oz (25 g) Parmesan cheese
flaky sea salt
freshly ground black pepper

▶ Preheat the oven to 400°F (200°C). Place the salmon in a baking dish. Cut off the wood-like bottom parts of the asparagus and place them in the dish with the salmon. Add the tomatoes and olives. Drizzle the oil on top. Bake in the oven for 20 minutes or until the salmon is cooked through.

Drizzle some extra olive oil on top of the vegetables, sprinkle some salt on top, and grate the parmesan over it all.

Asparagus is a super food! Twelve asparagus stalks provide the daily recommended intake of folic acid, which is something most people eat too little of. They are also a good source of vitamin C and antioxidants, so you can enjoy this recipe guilt-free. Make sure the olives are kalamata or another type of authentic black olive. You should never purchase olives that have been dyed black with ferric oxide. Not only are they not as healthy, but who wants to eat ferric oxide?

Cod on a Bed of Greens

4 servings

1¾ lbs (800 g) cod fillet
2 tbsp salt
5 white peppercorns
17⅔ oz (500 g) savoy cabbage
1 organic lemon, zest
4 tbsp olive oil
4 hardboiled eggs
salt
freshly ground black pepper

Horseradish Yogurt
¾ cup (200 ml) Greek yogurt
2 tbsp mayonnaise
2 tbsp freshly grated horseradish
salt
freshly ground black pepper

▶ Place the fish in a wide saucepan and pour in enough water to completely submerse the fish. Add the salt and white peppercorns. Bring to a boil, reduce heat immediately, and let simmer on low heat under a lid for about 5 minutes. The fish is supposed to become white and firm. Drain the water.

Finely shred the cabbage and fry in the oil along with the lemon zest for about 5 minutes. The cabbage is supposed to soften but shouldn't get any color. Add salt and pepper to taste.

Chop the hardboiled eggs.

Mix the ingredients for the horseradish yogurt and season with salt and pepper to taste.

Place the fish on a bed of cabbage and lastly, sprinkle the chopped eggs on top. Serve with the horseradish yogurt on the side.

Cod contains a relatively low amount of fat, but a rather large share of that fat consists of omega-3 fatty acids, so it's still a good ingredient from an LCHQ perspective. Research has also found that the consumption of cod makes it easier to lose weight, so it's good for your physical fitness to eat cod a couple of times a week. Savoy cabbage is one of the more flavorful types of cabbage and when it's cooked, the body can more easily absorb the nutrients than when consumed raw.

Cod with Garlic-fried Mushrooms and Quinoa

4 servings

1¾ lbs (800 g) cod fillet
3 tbsp olive oil
⅔ cup (150 g) black olives, preferably kalamata
1 red onion
3 garlic cloves
salt
freshly ground black pepper

Garlic-fried Mushrooms and Quinoa
½ cup (100 ml) uncooked quinoa
14 oz (400 g) Portobello mushroom
1 red onion
2 garlic cloves
3 tbsp olive oil
9 oz (250 g) cherry tomatoes
2½ oz (70 g) mixed lettuce, e.g., mache lettuce, baby spinach, arugula
salt
freshly ground black pepper

▶ Preheat the oven to 200°F (100°C). Place the fish in a baking dish. Drizzle with the olive oil and add salt and pepper. Chop the olives, onion, and garlic and place on top of the fish. Bake in the oven for 10–15 minutes, or until a digital thermometer reads an inner temperature of 149°F (65°C).

Cook the quinoa according to the directions on the packaging and add salt.

Rinse and dice the mushrooms, chop the onions and garlic. Fry the mushrooms and onion in oil for a couple of minutes in a frying pan until some of the liquid has evaporated. Add salt and pepper. Add the quinoa to the mushroom mix.

Split the cherry tomatoes and serve with the fish along with the lettuce and mushroom quinoa.

Kalamata olives are really good olives with lots of healthy monounsaturated fat and antioxidants. When you choose lettuce you should go for the leaves that have the most color, and preferably lots of it—that usually means it's the healthiest!

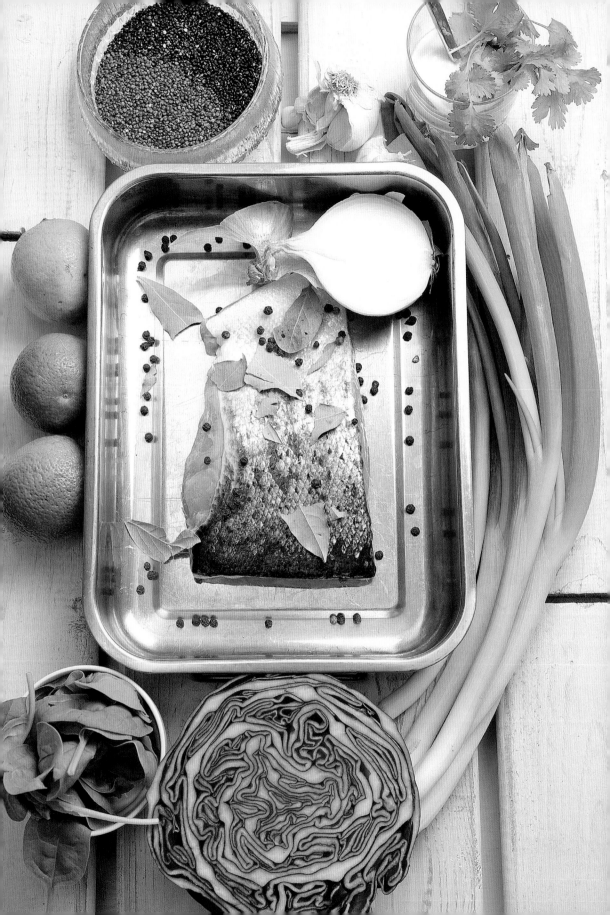

Poached Salmon with Quinoa and Cilantro Yogurt

4 servings

1⅓ lbs (600 g) salmon fillet
1 onion
4 cups (1 liter) water
1 tbsp salt
1 bay leaf
5 black peppercorns
2 tbsp white wine vinegar

Cilantro Yogurt
3/4 cup (200 ml) plain Greek yogurt
2 tbsp chopped fresh cilantro
2 garlic cloves, pressed
salt

Quinoa Salad
½ cup (100 ml) uncooked quinoa
14 oz (400 g) red cabbage
1 bunch of scallions
2½ oz (70 g) baby spinach
4 tbsp olive oil
2 tbsp freshly squeezed lime juice
salt
freshly ground black pepper

▶ Preheat the oven to 350°F (175°C). Place the salmon skin-side up in a baking dish. Peel and slice the onion. Bring the water to a boil along with the sliced onion, salt, bay leaf, black peppercorns, and vinegar. Pour the boiling water over the fish and place in the oven. Let the fish simmer for 15 minutes until it is cooked through. Make sure the water completely covers the fish.

Remove the dish from the oven and peel off the skin while the fish is still warm.

Mix all of the ingredients for the cilantro yogurt. Add salt to taste.

Cook the quinoa according to the directions on the packaging. Shred the red cabbage and scallions thinly. Mix the quinoa, cabbage, onion, and spinach. Add oil and freshly squeezed lime juice. Season with salt and pepper to taste.

Oven-baking the fish is much more gentle compared to, for example, frying or grilling. The results are also fantastically delicious! But even traditional oven-baking can give the fish a fried surface, which means that the omega-3 fats have been destroyed. Yogurt-based sauces are very good from an LCHQ perspective, since they provide both good fats and helpful bacteria.

Salmon Sashimi with Bok Choy and Pine Nuts

4 servings

1 (400 g) skinless, boneless salmon fillet, preferably sushi grade
28 oz (800 g) bok choy
⅓ cup (40 g) pine nuts
3 tbsp olive oil
3 garlic cloves, pressed

For serving
soy sauce
pickled ginger

▶ Cut the salmon fillet into thin slices. Separate the bok choy leaves and split the largest leaves vertically. Heat the oil in a frying pan. Add the pressed garlic and bok choy and fry at medium heat until the leaves have softened but have not yet obtained color. Roast the pine nuts briefly in a hot, non-stick frying pan until they obtain some color, but watch out—they burn easily!

Serve the salmon fillet with the fried cabbage and pine nuts. Soy and pickled ginger are great condiments.

Attention: It's vital that the salmon is completely fresh and doesn't contain any parasites. If you want to be extra sure, you should freeze the fish for at least 3 days beforehand.

Bok choy is a type of cabbage that is very healthy and when it is cooked, the body more easily absorbs the cancer inhibiting substances that hide in the leaves. This recipe has very low carbohydrate content and accords with the LCHQ philosophy of eating 20–30E% per day. If you eat this meal as dinner, there's still room for some fruit during earlier meals.

Almond-breaded Halibut with Hot Lentil Salad

4 servings

1 egg
½ cup (100 ml) almond flour
1 lb (400 g) halibut fillets (alt. flounder)
1 tbsp coconut oil
salt

Hot Lentil Salad
2 shallots
9 oz (250 g) cherry tomatoes
2 tbsp olive oil
11½ oz (400 ml) cooked green lentils
2½ oz (70 g) baby spinach
salt
freshly ground black pepper

Egg Sauce
¾ cup (200 ml) sour cream
2 hard boiled eggs, chopped
salt
freshly ground white pepper

▶ Crack the egg in a bowl and whisk with a fork. Spread out the almond flour on a plate. Dip the halibut fillets one by one, first in the egg and then in the flour. Heat the coconut oil in a frying pan and fry the fish fillets on both sides until they're cooked the whole way through. Add salt.

Peel and finely chop the onion and split the tomatoes. Heat the oil in a frying pan and fry the onion until it softens slightly. Add the cooked lentils and spinach and fry until the latter has wilted. Add the tomatoes and add salt and pepper to taste.

Mix all of the ingredients for the egg sauce and season with salt and pepper to taste.

Halibut is a medium fatty fish with about 3 percent fat, out of which a relatively large share is omega-3. Almond flour is a rather exclusive product, but is incredibly healthy with its low carb content and glycemic index. This is a top recipe from a LCHQ perspective and it's even great for those with a gluten intolerance.

Salmon with Ratatouille and Saffron Yogurt

4 servings

1⅓ lbs (600 g) salmon fillet
salt
freshly ground black pepper

Ratatouille
1 eggplant
1 squash
1 red bell pepper
1 onion
3 garlic cloves, pressed
3 tbsp olive oil
2 cups (500 g) crushed tomatoes
1 tbsp tomato puree
1 tsp honey
½ to a full pinch of cumin
¾ cup (200 ml) cooked white beans
salt
freshly ground black pepper

Saffron Yogurt
⅔ cup (150 ml) plain Greek yogurt
3½ tbsp (50 ml) mayonnaise
approx. half a packet of saffron (a pinch)
salt

▶ Preheat the oven to 400°F (200°C). Place the salmon skin-side up in a baking dish and bake in the oven for 15–20 minutes. Remove the salmon and peel off the skin while the fish is still hot. Add salt and pepper.

Dice the eggplant, squash, and bell pepper, peel and cut the onion into wedges. Heat the oil in a large saucepan or frying pan and fry the vegetables for approximately 5 minutes until they become soft without changing color. Pour in the crushed tomatoes, tomato puree, honey, and spices, and let simmer slightly for about 10 minutes. Add the beans and then season to taste with salt and pepper.

Mix all of the ingredients for the saffron yogurt and add salt to taste.

Serve the salmon with the ratatouille and saffron yogurt.

Ratatouille is the ultimate form of cooked vegetables. It not only contains a good variety, it's also insanely delicious! In principle, you can eat as much as you want of it without getting a caloric surplus. Saffron is packed with antioxidants, which have been proven to prevent depression, and not to mention how delicious the saffron makes this dish.

LCHQ

MEAT AND POULTRY

Lamb Kebob Red and White

Oven-baked Chicken with Root Vegetables and Feta

Chicken with Indian Vegetable Casserole

Chicken Burger with a Kick

Venison Burgers with Fried Onion Rings

Lamb Patties with Melon and Feta Salad

Chicken Stir Fry with Cashews

Chicken with Bulgur and Mint Yogurt

Venison with Cauliflower Mash and Cranberries

Pork Stir Fry

Lamb Kebob Red and White

4 servings

1 onion
1 lb (500 g) ground lamb
2 garlic cloves, pressed
1 tsp salt
1 tsp ground cumin
1 tsp ground cilantro
½ tsp ground cinnamon
½ tsp chili pepper
2 tbsp canola oil

Yogurt Sauce
¾ cup (200 ml) Greek yogurt
1 tbsp mayonnaise
1 garlic clove, pressed
2 tbsp freshly chopped cilantro
salt

Spicy Tomato Sauce
1 onion
3 tbsp olive oil
2 garlic cloves, pressed
1 can of crushed tomatoes
(14 oz [400 g])
3 tbsp tomato puree
1 tbsp red wine vinegar
2 tsp honey
½–1 tsp chili pepper
salt
freshly ground black pepper

Mixed Salad
1 red onion
1 cucumber
10½ oz (300 g) tomatoes
1 small head of iceberg lettuce
2 tbsp olive oil
1 tbsp red wine vinegar
herb salt (such as Tuscan)

▶ Peel and chop the onion. Mix the ground lamb, garlic, salt, cumin, cilantro, cinnamon, chili pepper, and onion. Form eight oblong sausages and fry in oil in a pan for about 5–7 minutes or until they are cooked the whole way through.

Mix the ingredients for the yogurt sauce and add salt to taste.

Peel and chop the onion for the tomato sauce. Heat oil in a saucepan, and then add the onion and garlic and fry for a couple of minutes without letting it change color. Add the crushed tomatoes, tomato puree, vinegar, honey, and chili pepper. Bring to a boil and let it boil gently for about 10 minutes. Season with salt and pepper to taste.

Peel and thinly slice the onion for the salad. Dice the cucumber and tomatoes. Mix the onion with the cucumber and tomatoes and add the oil, vinegar, and herb salt.

Place pieces of lettuce on plates. Distribute the salad on top and top off with the meat.

This recipe has many health benefits in the forms of probiotics from the yogurt, anti-oxidants from the tomato sauce and salad, as well as good fats from the lamb. If not all of your dinner guests follow LCHQ, you can serve pita bread on the side.

Oven-baked Chicken with Root Vegetables and Feta

4 servings

28 oz (800 g) kohlrabi
14 oz (400 g) red beets
10½ oz (300 g) parsley root
1 organic lemon
4 chicken drumsticks with skin (approx. 2 lbs [1 kg])
4 tbsp olive oil
2 tsp dried herbs, e.g., oregano, thyme, basil, rosemary, or marjoram
10½ oz (300 g) cherry tomatoes
20 olives, preferably kalamata
salt
freshly ground black pepper

For serving
⅔ cup (150 g) feta cheese
fresh thyme

▶ Preheat the oven to 450°F (225°C). Peel and dice the kohlrabi, beets, and parsley root. Halve the lemon and cut one of the halves in wedges. Place the root vegetables and lemon wedges in a baking dish, along with the chicken drumsticks, and add the olive oil, juice from the remaining lemon half, dried herbs, salt, and pepper. With your hands, rub the oil and spices into the chicken. Bake in the oven for 30 minutes. Add the tomatoes and olives and bake for another 10 minutes.

Sprinkle the feta cheese on top and garnish with fresh thyme.

Here we are using the root vegetables with the lowest carbohydrate count, which means you can eat a lot without consuming too many calories and carbohydrates. Feta cheese is the perfect flavoring and it has actually been proven that dairy products are better for your weight and cardiovascular health than previously believed. This is due to the amount of monounsaturated fat and short and medium-chained saturated fats (SCT and MCT). In addition, dairy products contain a lot of calcium and protein, which is beneficial for your health and overall fitness.

Chicken with Indian Vegetable Casserole

4 servings

1 lb (500 g) chicken fillets
1 onion
2 carrots
10½ oz (300 g) cabbage
4 tbsp olive oil
2 garlic cloves, pressed
1 tsp curry powder
1 tsp ground ginger
1 tsp turmeric
17¾ oz (500 g) crushed tomatoes
2 tbsp concentrated vegetable stock
7 oz (200 g) mushrooms
¾ cup (200 ml) cooked chickpeas, rinsed
1 tsp honey
salt
freshly ground black pepper

For serving
4 tbsp Greek yogurt

▶ Preheat the oven to 400°F (200°C). Place the chicken fillets in a baking dish, add salt and pepper, and bake in the oven for 20–25 minutes until they are cooked through.

Peel and chop the onion, peel and slice the carrots into coins, and shred the cabbage.

Heat the oil in a saucepan, add the onion, garlic, cabbage, carrots, and spices and fry for about 5 minutes. Add the crushed tomatoes and stock, and let simmer for 15 minutes. Add the mushrooms, the chickpeas, and honey and let boil lightly for another 5 minutes. Add salt and pepper to taste.

Slice the chicken fillets and serve alongside the vegetable casserole and a dollop of yogurt.

Curry is a wonderful spice mix full of turmeric. It has an anti-inflammatory effect, which has been found to relax the digestive system. It is, of course, the turmeric that generates that nice yellow color. The chickpeas don't just add carbohydrates, but also lots of fiber and antioxidants.

Chicken Burger with a Kick

4 servings

1⅓ lb (600 g) chicken thigh fillets
1 stalk of lemongrass
1 tsp salt
a pinch of black pepper
1 tbsp coconut oil
1 head of iceberg lettuce
4 tomatoes
1 red onion

Cilantro Yogurt
1¼ cup (300 ml) plain Greek yogurt
3 tbsp freshly chopped cilantro
1–2 garlic cloves, pressed
salt

For serving
sambal oelek

▶ Pound the hard part of the lemongrass stalk and then finely chop it. Add the pieces of chicken, a couple at a time, along with the lemongrass, salt, and pepper in a food processor and grind until it becomes forcemeat. Form the forcemeat into 8 small burgers. Fry them in coconut oil in a frying pan at medium heat for about 6 minutes per side, or until they are cooked the whole way through.

Mix all of the ingredients for the cilantro yogurt and add salt to taste.

Slice the tomatoes and red onion. Split the lettuce head into large leaves. Place each burger on a piece of lettuce, top off with tomato and onion slices, cilantro yogurt, and some sambal oelek. Fold.

Black peppercorns are extremely rich in antioxidants and new research has found that they appear to increase the energy expenditure and fat burning process. Sambal oelek has similar properties.

Venison Burgers with Fried Onion Rings

4 servings

1 lb (500 g) ground venison
1 egg yolk
1 tsp salt
1 tsp ground black pepper
2 onions
2 tomatoes
1 tbsp coconut oil
4 slices of aged cheese, such as cheddar
1 head of iceberg lettuce
2 tbsp mayonnaise

▶ Place the ground venison in a bowl and mix with the egg yolk, salt, and pepper. Form 4 burgers. Peel and slice the onions into rings. Slice the tomatoes.

Fry the onion rings in a frying pan with ½ tbsp coconut oil for about 10 minutes until the onions become soft and golden, but be careful that they don't burn. Fry the burgers in ½ tbsp coconut oil in a frying pan for a couple of minutes on each side until they are cooked the whole way through. Place a slice of cheese on each burger.

Place a couple of pieces of lettuce on top of the burgers along with the onion rings, slices of tomato, and top off with a dab of mayonnaise. Fold the leaves, and eat with your hands.

A perfectly filling dinner with few calories. Game is much healthier than livestock since it contains less fat, and the fat it does contain is of much better quality than in other types of meat. Mayonnaise, especially the homemade kind, is actually a decent source of fat since it is based with canola oil.

Lamb Patties with Melon and Feta Salad

4 servings

1 lb (500 g) ground lamb meat
4 garlic cloves, pressed
1 tsp salt
2 pinches of ground black pepper
1 tsp dried Herbes de provence (spice mix)
3½ tbsp (50 ml) finely chopped parsley
2 tbsp olive oil

Melon and Feta Salad
1 lb (500 g) watermelon
⅔ cup (150 g) feta cheese
9 oz (250 g) cherry tomatoes
1 red onion
5⅓ oz (150 g) mixed green lettuce
1 can of black beans (14 oz [400 g])
2 tbsp olive oil
½ tbsp white wine vinegar
salt
freshly ground black pepper

▶ Mix the ground meat with the garlic, spices, and parsley. Sear the patties in oil at a high temperature, then reduce to medium heat, and fry the patties until they are cooked the whole way through.

Dice the watermelon and feta cheese, split the tomatoes, and peel and thinly slice the onion. Place the pieces of lettuce on a tray, top with melon, cheese, tomatoes, onion, and beans. Pour oil and vinegar on top and add salt and pepper just before serving.

Ground lamb has a decent fat composition and is significantly more flavorful than ground beef. This recipe combines some of our favorite ingredients as well as vegetables and fruits. It also has a slightly high carbohydrate content, primarily because of the watermelon, which makes it a perfect post-workout meal when your need for carbohydrates is high.

Chicken Stir Fry with Cashews

4 servings

1 lb (500 g) chicken thigh fillets
14 oz (400 g) cabbage
10½ oz (300 g) broccoli
9 oz (250 g) carrots
7 oz (200 g) shitake mushrooms
1 piece of fresh ginger (approx. 2 inches [5 cm])
2 garlic cloves, pressed
½ cup (200 ml) plain cashews
4 tbsp canola oil

Soy and Sesame Sauce
3 tbsp soy sauce
1 tbsp sesame oil
2 tsp honey
2 tsp rice vinegar
1 tbsp sesame seeds

▶ Cut the chicken fillets into bite-sized pieces. Chop the cabbage, cut the broccoli into small florets, and peel and cut the carrots into sticks. Split the mushrooms; peel and finely chop the ginger.

Mix all of the ingredients for the sauce.

Heat 2 tbsp of oil in a frying pan, add the garlic and ginger, along with the chicken and fry until it is cooked the whole way through. Remove the chicken from the pan. Heat an additional 2 tbsp of oil in the frying pan and add the rest of the vegetables. Fry until they have become slightly soft. Add the sauce, chicken, and nuts. Stir and heat up everything together.

Chicken thigh fillets contain slightly more fat and are tastier than chicken breasts. Since the fat quality is decent, it is a great alternative. This recipe also uses a lot of vegetables, which are not only good for your body, but have a low calorie count so you can eat as much as you want. The cashews contribute with a low glycemic index and a lot of flavor.

Chicken with Bulgur and Mint Yogurt

4 servings

1¾ lbs (800 g) chicken fillet
2 tbsp olive oil
½ lemon, juice
salt
freshly ground black pepper

Bulgur Salad
½ cup (100 ml) uncooked whole grain bulgur
9 oz (250 g) cherry tomatoes
1 red onion
3½ oz (100 g) mixed green lettuce
2 tbsp olive oil
½ tbsp red wine vinegar
1 organic lemon, zest
salt
freshly ground black pepper

Mint Yogurt
¾ cup (200 ml) Greek yogurt
1 tbsp chopped fresh mint
1 garlic clove, pressed
salt
freshly ground white pepper

▶ Preheat the oven to 400°F (200°C). Rub the chicken fillets with the oil and lemon juice and add salt and pepper. Place them in a baking dish and bake in the oven for 20–25 minutes until the chicken is cooked through.

Cook the bulgur according to the instructions on the package. Split the tomatoes and peel and finely chop the onion. Mix the vegetables and bulgur, then add the oil and vinegar. Season with salt and black pepper to taste. Mix the ingredients for the mint yogurt, and then add salt and pepper to taste.

Whole grain bulgur consists of whole wheat grains that have been rolled but still maintain the nutritious inner shell. That makes whole grain bulgur a healthy, nutritious, and low glycemic alternative to other sources of carbohydrates. This recipe, along with many more in this book, contains olive oil. This wasn't chosen randomly, since it is one of the healthiest oils that exists and has a naturally anti-inflammatory effect.

Venison with Cauliflower Mash and Cranberries

4 servings

4 scallions
7 oz (200 g) chanterelles, fresh or frozen
1 lb (500 g) frozen, shredded venison
1 tbsp coconut oil
⅔ cup (150 ml) cranberries
salt
freshly ground black pepper

Cauliflower Mash
1⅓ lb (600 g) cauliflower
approx. ½ cup (100 ml) milk
4 tbsp cheddar or Parmesan cheese
salt
freshly ground black pepper

▶ Bring salted water to a boil. Split the cauliflower into florets and boil until they have softened. Mash the cauliflower, add milk until you reach the desired texture, add the cheese, and add salt and pepper to taste.

Peel and finely chop the onion. Rinse and cut the larger mushrooms into smaller pieces.

Cut the half-frozen meat into smaller pieces (if the venison isn't pre-shredded, now is a good time to shred it). Heat ½ tbsp coconut oil in a frying pan and fry the onion and mushrooms for a couple of minutes. Remove the mushroom mixture. Heat the rest of the coconut oil in a frying pan and add the venison. Fry until it browns. Add the fried mushroom mixture and cranberries and combine. If you're using frozen cranberries, you can sweeten them with a little bit of honey.

Game contains both less and better fat than beef. It also doesn't have the inflammatory effect that beef can have.

101

Pork Stir Fry

4 servings

10½ oz (300 g) eggplant
10½ oz (300 g) squash
1 red bell pepper
10½ oz (300 g) Chinese lettuce (alt. Swiss chard or spinach leaves)
7 oz (200 g) mushrooms, e.g., chanterelle or shiitake
½ tbsp coconut oil
1 lb (400 g) pork tenderloin
2 tbsp canola oil
1 tsp freshly ground ginger
2 garlic cloves, pressed
1–2 tsp sambal oelek
salt
freshly ground black pepper

▶ Dice the eggplant, squash, and bell pepper, shred the lettuce and slice the mushrooms.

Heat the coconut oil in a frying pan. Sear the pork tenderloin and shred it into small pieces. Heat the oil in a pan, add the ginger, garlic, egg plant, squash, and mushrooms and fry for a couple of minutes. Then add the lettuce and bell pepper; fry for a little while longer. Add sambal oelek, salt, and pepper to taste. Garnish with fresh herbs, such as basil, parsley, or cilantro.

Coconut oil is interesting since its reputation has completely changed in recent years. It contains 60–70 percent short and medium-chained saturated fats and they don't behave at all like their long relatives that exist in fatty meat products. The short and medium-chained saturated fats are barely stored as body fat and are easy for the body to use as fuel.

LCHQ

OMELETS
AND
VEGETARIAN
MEALS

Omelet with Cheese and Vegetables

Asian Omelet with Shrimp and Mushrooms

Turkey, Arugula, and Mozzarella Omelet

Falafel with Salad and Mint Tzatziki

Omelet with Cheese and Vegetables

4 servings

1 onion
9 oz (250 g) chanterelle mushrooms
8 eggs
2 tbsp water
20 green olives, sliced
¾ cup (200 ml) grated cheese
1 tsp salt
4 tbsp olive oil
7 oz (200 g) tomatoes
freshly ground black pepper

For serving
marinated artichokes
mixed lettuce, e.g., arugula, iceberg lettuce, and baby spinach

▶ Peel and chop the onion and slice the mushrooms. Whisk the eggs lightly with a fork, and then add water, olives, grated cheese, and salt.

Heat 2 tablespoons of oil in a frying pan, fry the onion and mushrooms until the liquid has evaporated. Add pepper to taste. Put half of the mixture aside. Add another tablespoon of oil to the pan with the mushrooms and pour in the egg batter. Lower the heat slightly and let the omelet cook slowly until it solidifies. Occasionally poke it with a spatula so that the batter seeps through.

Chop the tomatoes and add half of them to the omelet before it completely solidifies.

Place the omelet on a plate and make a second omelet with the rest of the ingredients. Serve with marinated artichokes and a green salad.

Despite being cheap, nutritious, and easy to cook, omelets are an underrated meal. This wonderfully flavorful omelet has a good range of vegetables. When preparing, it's best to use omega-3 eggs, because they contain an elevated level of omega-3 due to the fact that the chickens are fed flaxseed.

Asian Omelet with Shrimp and Mushrooms

2 servings

3½ oz (100 g) shiitake mushrooms
2 scallion stalks
1 red bell pepper
½–1 red chili pepper
5 eggs
3½ oz (100 g) pickled, peeled shrimp, rinsed
3 tbsp canola oil
1 tsp Thai fish sauce
salt
freshly ground black pepper

▶ Slice the mushrooms, thinly shred the scallions, and dice the bell pepper. Split the chili, scrape out the seeds, and thinly slice it. Use a half or whole pepper depending on desired heat. Feel free to keep the seeds if you want a really spicy dish.

Crack the eggs into a bowl and whisk with a fork. Add the bell pepper, scallions, chili pepper, and fish sauce.

Heat the oil in a frying pan, add the mushrooms and fry for about 1 minute until the mushrooms have softened and shrunk. Add the egg batter. Let the omelet solidify at medium temperature. Shake the frying pan slightly so that the omelet doesn't burn. When it is almost completely solid, add the shrimp and let them heat until the omelet is done. Add salt and pepper.

This is one of the most low-carb LCHQ recipes in this book and is therefore great for dinner. With really flavorful ingredients such as shrimp and shiitake mushrooms it is also an incredibly delicious meal.

Turkey, Arugula, and Mozzarella Omelet

2 servings

2 scallion stalks
¼ lb (100 g) turkey breast
3½ oz (100 g) cherry tomatoes
1¾ oz (50 g) mozzarella
2 tbsp olive oil
5 eggs
1 tbsp fresh, chopped basil
a pinch of salt
1¾ oz (50 g) arugula
freshly ground black pepper

▶ Peel and chop the onion, dice the turkey breast, split the tomatoes, and thinly slice the mozzarella. Heat the oil in a frying pan, add the onion and turkey, and sear the meat until it is halfway done. Crack the eggs in a bowl, add the basil and the salt and whisk lightly with a fork.

Add the egg batter to a frying pan and let solidify at medium heat. When the omelet is almost done, add the tomatoes and mozzarella. Sprinkle ground pepper on top. Top with arugula before serving.

Turkey meat is lean, flavorful, and filling, and is therefore great for myriad purposes. Here it appears in an omelet that takes only minutes to cook, but fully embraces the LCHQ philosophy.

LCHQ

DESSERTS

Coconut Ice Cream with Raspberry Sauce and Dark Chocolate

Strawberry Salad with Yogurt, Honey, and Walnuts

Coconut Panna Cotta with Lemongrass, Lime, and Passion Fruit

Silver Dollar Pancakes with Almond Flour and Lemon Cottage Cheese

Chocolate and Strawberry Milkshake

Coconut Ice Cream with Raspberry Sauce and Dark Chocolate

4 servings

1 egg white
9 oz (250 g) cottage cheese
3½ tbsp (50 ml) coconut milk
3 tbsp coconut flakes
1 tsp acacia honey

For serving
¾ cup (200 ml) raspberries
3 oz (80 g) dark chocolate (80% cocoa)

▶ Beat the eggs with an electric mixer until hard peaks form. Add the cottage cheese, coconut milk, coconut flakes, and honey while stirring continuously. Pour into a freezer safe container and freeze for about 1 hour. Stir occasionally so it doesn't completely solidify. You can also choose to run the mixture in an ice cream machine for a uniform consistency.

Mix the raspberries in a food processor. Melt the chocolate over boiling water and create chocolate shapes on a baking sheet; let them harden. Serve the ice cream with the raspberry sauce and chocolate shapes.

Isn't it wonderful when desserts are really healthy? You can easily eat this as a snack and your health would only benefit.

Strawberry Salad with Yogurt, Honey, and Walnuts

4 servings

10½ oz (300 g) strawberries
20 mint leaves
10½ oz (300 ml) Greek yogurt
1½ tbsp acacia honey
¾ cup (100 g) walnut halves

▶ Dice the strawberries and finely chop the mint leaves. Mix the berries and leaves, and pour the mixture into the bottom of four small, transparent glasses. Fill with yogurt, drizzle with honey, and top with walnuts.

Honey has continuously proven to be better for you than sugar. It contains a lower glycemic index, contributes with probiotics, contains antioxidants, and has a lower calorie count. Interestingly, it also contributes to higher levels of vitamins and minerals in the blood without actually containing any of those nutrients. It is unclear why, but perhaps the healthy bacteria facilitate the absorption of nutrients.

Coconut Panna Cotta with Lemongrass, Lime, and Passion Fruit

4 servings

2 sheets of gelatin
1 stalk of lemongrass
2 cups (500 ml) creamy coconut milk, 20%
2 tsp acacia honey
1 lime, zest
4 large passion fruits

▶ Soak the gelatin sheets in water for at least 5 minutes. Crush the lower part of the lemongrass and split the stalk. Add the coconut milk to a saucepan along with the lemongrass and honey. Bring to a boil and let simmer at a low temperature for a couple of minutes. Remove from the heat, then add the lime peel and gelatin sheets one at a time. Let cool. Remove the lemongrass, pour into 4 glasses, and place in the freezer for a couple of hours until they harden. Split the passion fruits and scrape out the flesh. Pour over the panna cotta.

Gelatin contains the amino acid hydroxyproline, which is a building block for your articular cartilage. This is why gelatin is sometimes helpful for people with osteoarthritis, and can possibly even help prevent it. Besides that, passion fruit is one of the most fiber rich fruits there is!

Silver Dollar Pancakes with Almond Flour and Lemon Cottage Cheese

4 pancakes

1 egg
1 cup (250 ml) milk, 1%
½ cup (125 ml) almond flour
½ tbsp psyllium husk
½ tsp salt
coconut oil for frying

Lemon Cottage Cheese
9 oz (250 g) cottage cheese
1 tbsp honey
1 organic lemon, zest

For serving
fresh berries

▶ Mix all of the ingredients for the lemon cottage cheese.

Crack the egg in a bowl, add the milk, and lightly mix with a balloon whisk. Add the almond flour and psyllium husk, stir well, and let rise for about 10 minutes.

Fry the pancakes in a Teflon pan with coconut oil.

Serve the pancakes with the cottage cheese and fresh berries—preferably large blueberries.

How can something so delicious be both LCHQ and healthy? Well, the secret is in the ingredients, and the fact that almond flour is one of them. Using cottage cheese is also a great way to achieve a creamy texture and a fresh taste to a hearty dish.

Chocolate and Strawberry Milkshake

1 serving

3½ oz (100 g) cottage cheese
½ cup (100 ml) milk
½ cup (100 ml) frozen strawberries
¾ oz (20 g) dark chocolate (80% cocoa)

▶ Combine all of the ingredients in a blender until it becomes a smooth beverage. Serve immediately.

In reality, this is a fantastic protein drink with a LCHQ configuration. Thanks to the chocolate, it's also a high-quality source of antioxidants.

INDEX

Fredrik Paulún introduced the concept of the glycemic index to the Swedish populace at the end of the 1990s. He has worked with nutrition and dietetics for about 20 years and is one of the leading experts. He has helped many people achieve better health through his nutrition center, books, TV, and radio appearances, and last but not least, his thousands of lectures.

Karoliina Paulún is an author who focuses on food, health, and exercise. She contributed all the recipes for this book.

Karoliina and Fredrik have previously co-authored the book *Low Carb High Quality: Food for a Thinner, Healthier Life,* available in English from Skyhorse Publishing.

ACKNOWLEDGMENTS

Thank you, Adam, . . . for the taste tests!

For the loan of props, thanks to:
NK Glas Porslin & Kök, Stockholm
EKPR & Kommunikation, Stockholm
Indiska, Stockholm